Written by Brigitte Gandiol-Coppin
Illustrated by Dominique Thibault

JUV I 495
JHR

Editorial Consultant:
Jean-François Pousse,
Historian

ISBN 0-944589-24-3
First U.S. Publication 1989 by
Young Discovery Library
217 Main St. • Ossining, NY 10562

YOUNG DISCOVERY LIBRARY

Cathedrals:
Stone upon Stone

YOUNG DISCOVERY LIBRARY

A vast roof. Soaring towers. Glowing stained glass windows. Hundreds of statues. What a beautiful building! **This is the cathedral.**
It is the biggest and most important church in town. In the **Middle Ages** (from the fifth to the fifteenth century), cathedrals were built to hold all the townspeople.
It took 40 to 50 years to build one, sometimes more.

Most cathedrals built in the Middle Ages are still standing, as awesome now as ever.

The bishop was the religious leader of a large area.
He ruled from his *cathedra* (seat)...the cathedral. Like a lord, he set rules and had a court of advisers.

In the 12th and 13th centuries, towns grew larger. Walls were built around them to make the towns safer than castles.

Peasants farmed the land and brought their harvests to the market. Some of them moved to town and became merchants or craftsmen—goldsmiths, weavers, or butchers... They became wealthy and formed **guilds** to defend themselves against a powerful lord or bishop.

Peasants who lived near the town had better tools and more horses.

Sometimes the town would grow
too large for its cathedral.
Sometimes an old cathedral
would burn down. Then the
bishop and the townspeople
decided to build a new one.
But that cost a lot!
Where would they find the money?
A group of clergymen called the
Chapter was in charge of finances.
They could put a special tax on
things, such as butter or meat
sold at the market.

The Chapter organized processions through the countryside and made collections in the villages.
Some people gave money. Others gave a horse or a cart. A rich lord might give some land with trees to use for wood, or maybe a stone quarry.
The king and princes were also asked to help. Sometimes a bishop would give part of his income. Wealthy townspeople gave money or gifts, too.
Soon, the workers began to cut stones from the quarry. Each stonecutter marked his blocks with a special pattern, called **boasting**, so the master could count and check his work.

Meanwhile, part of the old church was torn down, but part of it was left standing so services could continue. The stones from the old church would be used to build the new cathedral.

The Chapter would hold a contest to choose an architect or master builder. Sometimes it hired a well-known master who would bring his own team of **masons**. Many masters started out as stone carvers or **masons** who became known and respected by all. They traveled across Europe to build churches and other buildings. When they died, they were sometimes buried in a church they had built.

Once the plans were drawn, laborers would dig trenches for the foundations.

A master builder knew stone-carving and woodworking as well as math and geometry.

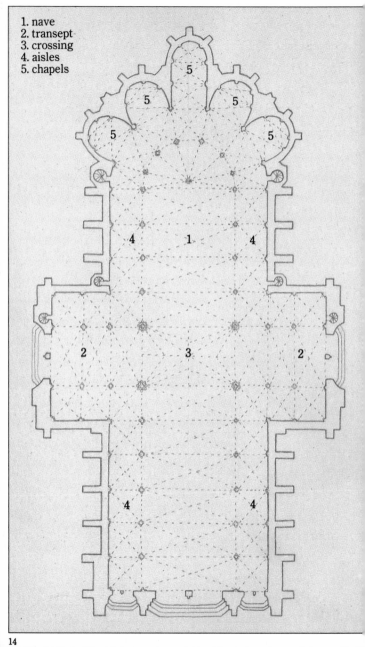

1. nave
2. transept
3. crossing
4. aisles
5. chapels

14

At the masons' lodge, **the master builder drew all the parts of the building**— pillars, arches, windows great and small—on wooden tablets or parchment.

Flying buttresses kept the walls from buckling under the thrust of the arches.

He got ideas from other churches, but he used his imagination, too. That is why all cathedrals look alike and different at the same time. **Flying butresses** made it possible to cut large windows and make the walls of the church thinner than before.

Great rose windows and tracery are typical of gothic-style cathedrals of the 13th century.

Meanwhile, woodcutters chopped down
tall trees to make beams for the
cathedral's frame.
**A lot of wood was used at the
building site** and the **joiners**
 were kept busy
making ladders,
scaffolding,
and hoists to lift
the stone. The stone blocks were brought
by wagon, or by ship if the
quarry was far away.
Winter was the best time to
cut trees. Oak wood was
preferred because it was
strong. Soaking it in
water first made it
even sturdier.

Stone was sent from the quarries to the building site, where **stone carvers** shaped the blocks with their chisels and mallets. Nearby, the **blacksmith** made all the iron tools that were needed to build the cathedral.

Shipping was very costly. It could double, or even triple, the price of materials.

Blacksmith   Joiners

The building site was a busy place.
Workers carried the stone blocks
to the masons in baskets and on
stretchers. The masons measured
the blocks so they would line
up perfectly. Then they spread
the mortar with trowels. They
used a plumb line to make sure
that the wall was straight.

Nearby, young helpers mixed
the mortar to hold the blocks.
One day the helpers would
be masons too.

Masons   Stone carvers

Carpenters

Workers were paid by the day or week. Most of them came from the town or nearby, except for the masons who spent their lives traveling from job to job. Work on the cathedral stopped in late autumn. The tops of the walls were covered with straw or manure to protect them from frost. The building site was idle until springtime.

Church roofs were often covered with sheets of lead.

Glassmakers melted sand and ashes in special ovens to make glass. When the glass was molten, they added colors.

The bishop and people from both town and country would often come to watch the work. They were proud of their new cathedral, which they had all helped to build. They wanted it to be the most beautiful cathedral in the land! For them, it was more than just a building: it was a sign of their bishop's power, and of Christianity. And, like the town halls that began to be built in the 13th century, it was a symbol of their community.

Building such a large structure was not easy. Sometimes there were failures. The architect who designed the cathedral of Beauvais wanted arches 145 feet high. But the weight was too much and the walls collapsed! The cathedral was never finished.

Pulleys and winches were used to hoist the stone up the walls.

While the cathedral slowly took shape, **glassmakers made the stained glass windows.** The pieces of colored glass were assembled like a puzzle and held together with strips of lead. A painter added details to them with a special gray paint called "grisaille." First he would add shadings to the figures' faces and clothing. Then he applied more grisaille to outline their eyes and noses. Finally, the decorated panels were set into the window frames.

The merchants' and craftsmen's guilds would pay large sums of money to have windows made for them in the new cathedral. That is why you can see stained glass pictures of goldsmiths and bakers alongside those of saints and apostles.

Have you ever been in a cathedral?
They are gigantic. Some of them are over 300 feet long and as much as 120 feet high—taller than a ten-story building.

The cathedral of Amiens (France) is one of the largest. It can hold 10,000 people!

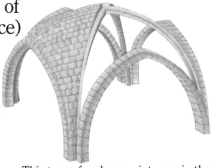

This type of arch came into use in the 12th century. Its four diagonal arches formed a vault, or roof.

Look at how these thin columns form enormous pillars to support the arcades. They then rise to meet the vaults of the cathedral ceiling.

Tall stained glass windows turn sunlight into rainbows. In the Middle Ages, the walls were hung with **tapestries**. Statues were painted with bright colors touched with gold.

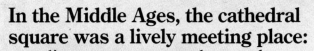

**In the Middle Ages, the cathedral
square was a lively meeting place:**
traveling actors put on plays and
peddlers displayed their wares.
The townspeople would meet there
to talk and to listen to sermons
and speeches.
The square was a good location
for stores—the shopping mall
of its time.

On **feast days**, joyous processions started at the cathedral. The people paraded through the town, singing and dancing. A feast could last for days if it was in honor of a saint who was special to the town. Today we still have the feasts of Easter and Christmas.

In his shop near the cathedral,
the goldsmith made jewelry for
princes, a silver chalice for the
bishop and religious articles
for the cathedral.
With an assistant and several
apprentices, the goldsmith
worked the gold and silver
with a mallet wrapped in a
rag. Then he would engrave
designs in the metal and set
it with precious stones. Each
goldsmiths' guild had its own
emblem. The London guild used
a leopard's head as its emblem.

The school was also near the cathedral.

Young men came to learn grammar and the Latin language. Latin was spoken by educated people in many countries. Religion and the writings of ancient Greek and Roman authors were important subjects.
The first universities were started in the 13th century. Large cities, like Paris in France and Bologna in Italy, had famous universities.
In the evening the students would gather in taverns to talk and drink, play music and make up songs.

The students used handwritten books and there might only be one in a class. Most was learned from the master, often a clergyman.

A few rich townspeople had houses built of stone. Most other people had wooden houses which caught on fire easily. On the ground floor of the houses were small open shops, warehouses, or stables. The upper floors had one or two rooms each, where whole families lived. You could tell what the shop sold by the picture sign in front.

Streets were narrow and rarely paved. When it rained, they turned to mud. Children played there alongside chickens, pigs and dogs. Carts could barely get through the crowd of beggars, peddlers, and gossiping shoppers. **There were no streetlamps.** At night, it was better to stay inside. Even though watchmen patrolled the streets, there might be evildoers and vagabonds hiding in the shadows.

Cathedral of Siena (Italy)

Cathedral of Leon (Spain) 13th-15th century

At last the cathedral was finished and was consecrated by the bishop or the pope in a grand ceremony. The cathedral was one of the most important buildings in the town. It was open to all people, not only for prayer, but also for lively discussion and amusements.

The cathedral of Albi (France), built in the 13th and 14th centuries, looked like a fortress.

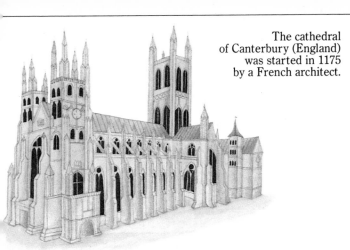

The cathedral of Canterbury (England) was started in 1175 by a French architect.

The first cathedrals were built in the large cities of France. Then the gothic style spread throughout Europe, especially England and Germany, but each country or region created its own style.

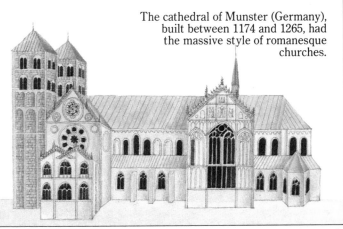

The cathedral of Munster (Germany), built between 1174 and 1265, had the massive style of romanesque churches.

35

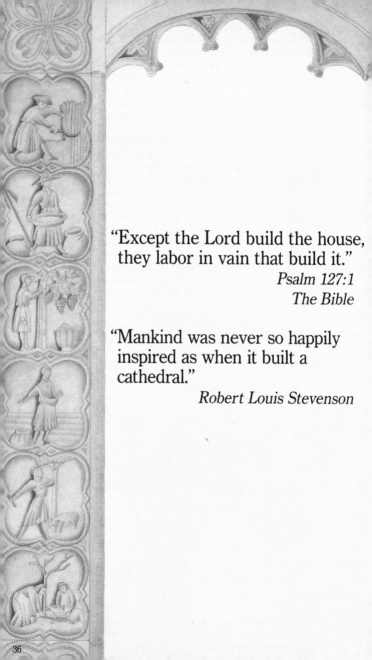

"Except the Lord build the house, they labor in vain that build it."
Psalm 127:1
The Bible

"Mankind was never so happily inspired as when it built a cathedral."

Robert Louis Stevenson

Index